let's cook

quick & easy

Sarah
Green

$\boxed{p}$

Contents

Easy Cheesy Risotto with Parmesan 4

Prawns (Shrimp) with Tomatoes 6

Quick Chicken Bake 8

Harlequin Chicken 10

Creamed Spaghetti & Mushrooms 12

Chorizo & Wild Mushrooms with a Spicy Vermicelli 14

Pasta Omlette 16

Egg Noodles with Beef 18

Vegetable Pasta Stir-fry 20

Potato & Bean Pâté 22

Potato Omlette with Feta Cheese & Spinach 24

Potato, Tomato & Sausage Panfry 26

Potato-Topped Cod 28

Four Cheese & Potato Layer Bake 30

Hummus 32

Baked Goat's Cheese Salad 34

Spanish Tortilla 36

Mediterranean Monkfish 38

Golden Chicken Pilau 40

Chicken with (Bell) Peppers & Black Bean Sauce 42

Spicy Chicken Tortillas 44

Neapolitan Pork Steaks 46

Easy Cheesy Risotto with Parmesan

Although this is the easiest, most basic risotto, it is one of the most delicious.
Because there are few ingredients, use the best of each.

Serves 4–6

INGREDIENTS

60–75 g/2–2³/₄ oz/4–5 tbsp unsalted butter
1 onion, finely chopped
300 g/10¹/₂ oz/1¹/₂ cups arborio or carnaroli rice

120 ml/4 fl oz/¹/₂ cup dry white vermouth or white wine
1.2 litres/2 pints/5 cups chicken or vegetable stock, simmering

80 g/3 oz/1 cup freshly grated Parmesan cheese, plus extra for sprinkling
salt and pepper

1 Heat about 25 g/1 oz/2 tbsp of the butter in a large heavy-based saucepan over a medium heat. Add the onion and cook for about 2 minutes until just beginning to soften. Add the rice and cook for about 2 minutes, stirring frequently, until translucent and well coated with the butter.

2 Pour in the vermouth: it will bubble and steam rapidly and evaporate almost immediately. Add a ladleful (about 225 ml/8 fl oz/1 cup) of the simmering stock and cook, stirring constantly, until the stock is absorbed.

3 Continue adding the stock, about half a ladleful at a time, allowing each addition to be absorbed before adding the next – never allow the rice to cook 'dry'. This should take 20–25 minutes. The risotto should have a creamy consistency and the rice grains should be tender, but still firm to the bite.

4 Remove the pan from the heat and stir in the remaining butter and Parmesan. Season with salt and a little pepper, to taste. Cover, stand for about 1 minute, then serve immediately with extra Parmesan for sprinkling.

COOK'S TIP

If you prefer not to use butter, soften the onion in 2 tablespoons olive oil and stir in about 2 tablespoons extra-virgin olive oil with the Parmesan at the end.

Prawns (Shrimp) with Tomatoes

Quick and easy to prepare, this dish is also extremely good to eat. Use the larger tiger prawns (shrimp) for special occasions, if you prefer.

Serves 4-6

INGREDIENTS

3 medium onions
1 green (bell) pepper
1 tsp fresh ginger root, finely
 chopped

1 tsp fresh garlic, crushed
1 tsp salt
1 tsp chilli powder
2 tbsp lemon juice

350 g/12 oz frozen prawns (shrimp)
3 tbsp oil
400 g/14 oz can tomatoes
fresh coriander (cilantro) leaves,
 to decorate

1 Using a sharp knife, slice the onions and the green (bell) pepper.

2 Place the ginger, garlic, salt and chilli powder in a small bowl and mix to combine. Add the lemon juice and mix to form a paste.

3 Place the prawns (shrimp) in a bowl of cold water and set aside to defrost. Drain thoroughly.

4 Heat the oil in a medium-sized saucepan. Add the onions and fry until golden brown.

5 Add the spice paste to the onions, reduce the heat to low and cook, stirring and mixing well, for about 3 minutes.

6 Add the tomatoes, tomato juice and the green (bell) pepper, and cook for 5-7 minutes, stirring occasionally.

7 Add the prawns (shrimp) to the pan and cook for 10 minutes, stirring occasionally. Garnish with fresh coriander (cilantro) leaves and serve hot with plain boiled rice and a crisp green salad.

COOK'S TIP

Fresh ginger root looks rather like a knobbly potato. The skin should be peeled, then the flesh either grated, finely chopped or sliced. Ginger is also available ground: this can be used as a substitute for fresh root ginger, but the fresh root is far superior.

Quick Chicken Bake

This recipe is a type of cottage pie and is just as versatile. Add vegetables and herbs of your choice, depending on what you have at hand.

Serves 4

INGREDIENTS

500 g/1 lb 2 oz minced (ground) chicken

1 large onion, chopped finely

2 carrots, diced finely

25 g/1 oz/2 tbsp plain (all-purpose) flour

1 tbsp tomato purée (paste)

300 ml/1^1/$_2$ pint/1^1/$_4$ cups chicken stock

pinch of fresh thyme

900 g/2 lb potatoes, creamed with butter and milk and highly seasoned

90 g/3 oz/^{3}/$_4$ cup grated Lancashire cheese

salt and pepper

peas, to serve

---

1 Dry-fry the minced (ground) chicken, onion and carrots in a non-stick saucepan for 5 minutes, stirring frequently.

2 Sprinkle the chicken with the flour and simmer for a further 2 minutes.

3 Gradually blend in the tomato purée (paste) and stock then simmer for 15 minutes. Season and add the thyme.

4 Transfer the chicken and vegetable mixture to an ovenproof casserole and allow to cool.

5 Spoon the mashed potato over the chicken mixture and sprinkle with the Lancashire cheese. Bake in a preheated oven, 200°C/400°F/Gas Mark 6, for 20 minutes, or until the cheese is bubbling and golden, then serve with the peas.

VARIATION

Instead of Lancashire cheese, you could sprinkle Cotswold cheese over the top. This is a tasty blend of Double Gloucester, onion and chives, and is ideal for melting as a topping. Alternatively, you could use a mixture of cheeses, depending on whatever you have at hand.

Harlequin Chicken

This colourful, simple dish will tempt the appetites of all the family – it is ideal for toddlers, who enjoy the fun shapes of the multi-coloured (bell) peppers.

Serves 4

INGREDIENTS

10 skinless, boneless chicken thighs
1 medium onion
1 each medium red, green
   and yellow (bell) peppers
1 tbsp sunflower oil

400 g/14 oz can chopped
   tomatoes
2 tbsp chopped fresh parsley
pepper

wholemeal (whole wheat) bread and
   a green salad, to serve

1 Using a sharp knife, cut the chicken thighs into bite-sized pieces.

2 Peel and thinly slice the onion. Halve and deseed the (bell) peppers and cut into small diamond shapes.

3 Heat the oil in a shallow frying pan (skillet). Add the chicken and onion and fry quickly until golden.

4 Add the (bell) peppers, cook for 2–3 minutes, then stir in the tomatoes and parsley and season with pepper.

5 Cover tightly and simmer for about 15 minutes, until the chicken and vegetables are tender. Serve hot with wholemeal (whole wheat) bread and a green salad.

COOK'S TIP

You can use dried parsley instead of fresh but remember that you only need about one half the quantity of dried to fresh.

COOK'S TIP

If you are making this dish for small children, the chicken can be finely chopped or minced (ground) first.

Creamed Spaghetti & Mushrooms

*This easy vegetarian dish is ideal for busy people
with little time, but good taste!*

Serves 4

INGREDIENTS

60 g/2 oz/4 tbsp butter
2 tbsp olive oil
6 shallots, sliced
450 g/1 lb/6 cups sliced
  button mushrooms
1 tsp plain (all purpose) flour

150 ml/^{1}/$_4$ pint/^{5}/$_8$ cup double
  (heavy) cream
2 tbsp port
115 g/4 oz sun-dried
  tomatoes, chopped
freshly grated nutmeg

450g /1 lb dried spaghetti
1 tbsp freshly chopped parsley
salt and pepper
6 triangles of fried white bread,
  to serve

1 Heat the butter and 1 tbsp of the oil in a large saucepan. Add the shallots and cook over a medium heat for 3 minutes. Add the mushrooms and cook over a low heat for 2 minutes. Season with salt and black pepper, sprinkle over the flour and cook, stirring constantly, for 1 minute.

2 Gradually stir in the cream and port, add the sun-dried tomatoes and a pinch of grated nutmeg and cook over a low heat for 8 minutes.

3 Meanwhile bring a large saucepan of lightly salted water to the boil. Add the spaghetti and remaining olive oil and cook for 12–14 minutes, until tender but still firm to the bite.

4 Drain the spaghetti and return to the pan. Pour over the mushroom sauce and cook for 3 minutes. Transfer the spaghetti and mushroom sauce to a large serving plate and sprinkle over the chopped parsley. Serve with crispy triangles of fried bread.

VARIATION

Non-vegetarians could add 115 g/ 4 oz Parma ham (prosciutto), cut into thin strips and heated gently in 25 g/1 oz/2 tbsp butter, to the pasta along with the mushroom sauce.

Chorizo & Wild Mushrooms with a Spicy Vermicelli

Simple and quick to make, this spicy dish will set the taste buds tingling.

Serves 6

INGREDIENTS

680 g/1¹/₂ lb dried vermicelli
125 ml/4 fl oz/¹/₂ cup olive oil
2 garlic cloves
125 g/4¹/₂ oz chorizo, sliced

225 g/8 oz wild mushrooms
3 fresh red chillies, chopped
2 tbsp freshly grated
  Parmesan cheese

salt and pepper
10 anchovy fillets, to garnish

---

1 Bring a large saucepan of lightly salted water to the boil. Add the vermicelli and 1 tbsp of the oil and cook until just tender, but still firm to the bite. Drain, place on a large, warm serving plate and keep warm.

2 Meanwhile heat the remaining oil in a large frying pan (skillet). Add the garlic and fry for 1 minute. Add the chorizo and wild mushrooms and cook for 4 minutes, then add the chopped chillies and cook for 1 further minute.

3 Pour the chorizo and wild mushroom mixture over the vermicelli and season with a little salt and pepper. Sprinkle over freshly grated Parmesan cheese, garnish with a lattice of anchovy fillets and serve immediately.

VARIATION

Fresh sardines may be used in this recipe in place of the anchovies. However, ensure that you gut and clean the sardines, removing the backbone, before using them.

COOK'S TIP

Always obtain wild mushrooms from a reliable source and never pick them yourself unless you are absolutely certain of their identity. Many varieties of mushrooms are now cultivated and most are virtually indistinguishable from the wild varieties. Mixed colour oyster mushrooms have been used here, but you could also use chanterelles. However, remember that chanterelles tend to shrink during cooking, so you may need more.

Pasta Omelette

This is a superb way of using up any leftover pasta,
such as penne, macaroni or conchiglie.

Serves 2

INGREDIENTS

4 tbsp olive oil
1 small onion, chopped
1 fennel bulb, thinly sliced
125 g/4$^{1}/_{2}$ oz potato, diced
1 garlic clove, chopped

4 eggs
1 tbsp chopped fresh flat leaf parsley
pinch of chilli powder
100 g/3$^{1}/_{2}$ oz cooked short pasta
2 tbsp stuffed green olives, halved

salt and pepper
fresh marjoram sprigs, to garnish
tomato salad, to serve

1 Heat half the oil in a heavy-based frying pan (skillet) over a low heat. Add the onion, fennel and potato and fry, stirring occasionally, for 8-10 minutes, until the potato is just tender.

2 Stir in the garlic and cook for 1 minute. Remove the pan from the heat and transfer the vegetables to a plate and set aside.

3 Beat the eggs until they are frothy. Stir in the parsley and season with salt, pepper and a pinch of chilli powder.

4 Heat 1 tbsp of the remaining oil in a clean frying pan (skillet). Add half of the egg mixture to the pan, then add the cooked vegetables, pasta and half of the olives. Pour in the remaining egg mixture and cook until the sides begin to set.

5 Lift up the edges of the omelette with a palette knife (spatula) to allow the uncooked egg to spread underneath. Cook, shaking the pan occasionally, until the underside is a light golden brown colour.

6 Slide the omelette out of the pan on to a plate. Wipe the pan with kitchen paper (kitchen towels) and heat the remaining oil. Invert the omelette into the pan and cook until the other side is golden brown.

7 Slide the omelette on to a warmed serving dish and garnish with the remaining olives and the marjoram. Serve cut into wedges, with a tomato salad.

Egg Noodles with Beef

Quick and easy, this mouth-watering Chinese-style noodle dish can be cooked in minutes.

Serves 4

INGREDIENTS

285 g/10 oz egg noodles
3 tbsp walnut oil
2.5 cm/1 inch piece fresh root ginger, cut into thin strips
5 spring onions (scallions), finely shredded
2 garlic cloves, finely chopped

1 red (bell) pepper, cored, seeded and thinly sliced
100 g/3$^{1}/_{2}$ oz button mushrooms, thinly sliced
340 g/12 oz fillet steak, cut into thin strips
1 tbsp cornflour (cornstarch)

5 tbsp dry sherry
3 tbsp soy sauce
1 tsp soft brown sugar
225 g/8 oz/1 cup beansprouts
1 tbsp sesame oil
salt and pepper
spring onion (scallion) strips, to garnish

1 Bring a large saucepan of water to the boil. Add the noodles and cook according to the instructions on the packet. Drain the noodles and set aside.

2 Heat the walnut oil in a preheated wok. Add the ginger, spring onions (scallions) and garlic and stir-fry for 45 seconds. Add the (bell) pepper, mushrooms and steak and stir-fry for 4 minutes. Season to taste with salt and pepper.

3 Mix together the cornflour (cornstarch), sherry and soy sauce in a small jug to form a paste, and pour into the wok. Sprinkle over the brown sugar and stir-fry all of the ingredients for a further 2 minutes.

4 Add the beansprouts, drained noodles and sesame oil to the wok, stir and toss together for 1 minute. Garnish with strips of spring onion (scallion) and serve immediately.

COOK'S TIP

If you do not have a wok, you could prepare this dish in a frying pan (skillet). However, a wok is preferable, as the round base ensures an even distribution of heat and it is easier to keep stirring and tossing the contents when stir-frying.

Vegetable Pasta Stir-fry

Prepare all the vegetables and cook the pasta in advance,
then the dish can be cooked in a few minutes.

Serves 4

INGREDIENTS

400 g/14 oz dried wholemeal (whole-wheat) pasta shells or other short pasta shapes
1 tbsp olive oil
2 carrots, thinly sliced
115 g/4 oz baby corn cobs
3 tbsp corn oil
2.5 cm/1 inch piece fresh root ginger, thinly sliced

1 large onion, thinly sliced
1 garlic clove, thinly sliced
3 celery sticks (stalks), thinly sliced
1 small red (bell) pepper, cored, seeded and cut into matchstick strips
1 small green (bell) pepper, cored, seeded and cut into matchstick strips

1 tsp cornflour (cornstarch)
2 tbsp water
3 tbsp soy sauce
3 tbsp dry sherry
1 tsp clear honey
a dash of hot pepper sauce (optional)
salt

1 Bring a large saucepan of lightly salted water to the boil. Add the pasta and olive oil and cook until tender, but still firm to the bite. Drain, return to the pan and keep warm.

2 Bring a saucepan of lightly salted water to the boil. Add the carrots and corn cobs and cook for 2 minutes. Drain, refresh in cold water and drain again.

3 Heat the corn oil in a preheated wok or large frying pan (skillet). Add the ginger and stir-fry over a medium heat for 1 minute to flavour the oil. Remove the ginger with a slotted spoon and discard.

4 Add the onion, garlic, celery and (bell) peppers to the pan and stir-fry for 2 minutes. Add the carrots and baby corn cobs and stir-fry for a further 2 minutes. Stir in the drained pasta.

5 Mix together the cornflour (cornstarch) and water to make a smooth paste. Stir in the soy sauce, sherry and honey. Pour the cornflour mixture into the pasta and cook, stirring occasionally, for 2 minutes. Stir in a dash of pepper sauce, if liked. Transfer to a serving dish and serve immediately.

Potato & Bean Pâté

This pâté is easy to prepare and may be stored in the refrigerator for up to two days. Serve with small toasts, Melba toast or crudités.

Serves 4

INGREDIENTS

100 g/3¹/₂ oz floury (mealy)
  potatoes, diced
225 g/8 oz mixed canned beans, such
  as borlotti, flageolet and kidney
  beans, drained

1 garlic clove, crushed
2 tsp lime juice
1 tbsp chopped fresh coriander
  (cilantro)
2 tbsp natural yogurt

salt and pepper
chopped fresh coriander (cilantro), to
  garnish

1 Cook the potatoes in a saucepan of boiling water for 10 minutes until tender. Drain well and mash.

2 Transfer the potato to a food processor or blender and add the beans, garlic, lime juice and the fresh coriander (cilantro). Season the mixture and process for 1 minute to make a smooth purée. Alternatively, mix the beans with the potato, garlic, lime juice and coriander (cilantro) and mash.

3 Turn the purée into a bowl and add the yogurt. Mix well.

4 Spoon the pâté into a serving dish and garnish with the chopped coriander (cilantro). Serve at once or leave to chill.

COOK'S TIP

To make Melba toast, toast ready-sliced white or brown bread lightly on both sides under a preheated high grill (broiler) and remove the crusts. Holding the bread flat, slide a sharp knife between the toasted bread to split it horizontally. Cut into triangles and toast the untoasted side until the edges curl.

VARIATION

If you do not have a food processor or you would prefer to make a chunkier pâté, simply mash the ingredients with a fork.

Potato Omelette with Feta Cheese & Spinach

This quick chunky omelette has pieces of potato cooked into the egg mixture and is then folded and filled with a classic combination of feta cheese and spinach.

Serves 4

INGREDIENTS

75 g/3 oz/^{1}/$_3$ cup butter
6 waxy potatoes, diced
3 garlic cloves, crushed
1 tsp paprika
2 tomatoes, skinned, seeded and diced

12 eggs
pepper

FILLING:
225 g/8 oz baby spinach

1 tsp fennel seeds
125 g/4^1/$_2$ oz feta cheese, diced
4 tbsp natural yogurt

1 Heat 2 tbsp of the butter in a frying pan (skillet) and cook the potatoes over a low heat for 7-10 minutes until golden, stirring constantly. Transfer to a bowl.

2 Add the garlic, paprika and tomatoes and cook for a further 2 minutes.

3 Whisk the eggs together in a jug and season with pepper. Pour the eggs into the potatoes and mix well.

4 Place the spinach in boiling water for 1 minute until just wilted. Drain and refresh the spinach under cold running water and pat dry with paper towels. Stir in the fennel seeds, feta cheese and yogurt.

5 Heat 1 tbsp of the butter in a 15 cm/6 inch omelette or frying pan (skillet). Ladle a quarter of the egg and potato mixture into the pan. Cook for 2 minutes, turning once, until set.

6 Transfer the omelette to a serving plate. Spoon a quarter of the spinach mixture on to one half of the omelette, then fold the omelette in half over the filling. Repeat to make 4 omelettes.

VARIATION

Use any other cheese, such as blue cheese, instead of the feta and blanched broccoli in place of the baby spinach, if you prefer.

Potato, Tomato & Sausage Panfry

This is a very simple dish which is delicious as a main meal. Choose good sausages flavoured either with herbs or use one of the many types of flavoured sausages, such as mustard or leek.

Serves 4

INGREDIENTS

2 large potatoes, sliced
1 tbsp vegetable oil
8 flavoured sausages
1 red onion, cut into 8
1 tbsp tomato purée (paste)

150 ml/^{1}/$_4$ pint/^{2}/$_3$ cup red wine
150 ml/^{1}/$_4$ pint/^{2}/$_3$ cup passata
2 large tomatoes, each cut into 8
175 g/6 oz broccoli florets,
   blanched

2 tbsp chopped fresh basil
salt and pepper
shredded fresh basil, to garnish

1 Cook the sliced potatoes in a saucepan of boiling water for 7 minutes. Drain thoroughly and set aside.

2 Meanwhile, heat the oil in a large frying pan (skillet). Add the sausages and cook for 5 minutes, turning the sausages frequently to ensure that they are browned on all sides.

3 Add the onion pieces to the pan and continue to cook for a further 5 minutes, stirring the mixture frequently.

4 Stir in the tomato purée (paste), red wine and the passata and mix together well. Add the tomato wedges, broccoli florets and chopped basil to the panfry and mix carefully.

5 Add the parboiled potato slices to the pan. Cook the mixture for about 10 minutes or until the sausages are completely cooked through. Season to taste with salt and pepper.

6 Garnish the panfry with fresh shredded basil and serve hot.

VARIATION

Broccoli is particularly good in this dish as it adds a splash of colour, but other vegetables of your choice can be used instead, if preferred.

COOK'S TIP

Omit the passata from this recipe and use canned plum tomatoes or chopped tomatoes for convenience.

Potato-Topped Cod

This simple dish has a spicy breadcrumb mixture topping layers of cod and potatoes. It is cooked in the oven until crisp and golden.

Serves 4

INGREDIENTS

60 g/2 oz/^{1}/$_4$ cup butter
4 waxy potatoes, sliced
1 large onion, finely chopped
1 tsp wholegrain mustard
1 tsp garam masala

pinch of chilli powder
1 tbsp chopped fresh dill
75 g/2^3/$_4$ oz/1^1/$_4$ cups fresh
  breadcrumbs

4 cod fillets, about 175 g/6 oz each
50 g/1^3/$_4$ oz Gruyère cheese, grated
salt and pepper
fresh dill sprigs, to garnish

1 Melt half of the butter in a frying pan (skillet). Add the potatoes and fry for 5 minutes, turning until they are browned all over. Remove the potatoes from the pan with a perforated spoon.

2 Add the remaining butter to the frying pan (skillet) and stir in the onion, mustard, garam masala, chilli powder, chopped dill and breadcrumbs. Cook for 1-2 minutes, stirring and mixing well.

3 Layer half of the potatoes in the base of an ovenproof dish and place the cod fillets on top. Cover the cod fillets with the rest of the potato slices. Season to taste with salt and pepper.

4 Spoon the spicy mixture from the frying pan (skillet) over the potato and sprinkle with the grated cheese.

5 Cook in a preheated oven, 200°C/400°F/Gas Mark 6, for 20-25 minutes or until the topping is golden and crisp and the fish is cooked through. Garnish with fresh dill sprigs and serve at once.

VARIATION

You can use any fish for this recipe: for special occasions use salmon steaks or fillets.

COOK'S TIP

This dish is ideal served with baked vegetables which can be cooked in the oven at the same time.

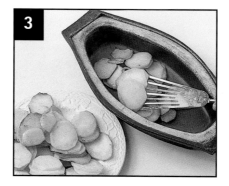

Four Cheese & Potato Layer Bake

This is a quick dish to prepare and it can be left to cook in the oven without requiring any further attention. Vary the combination of hard cheeses and vegetables according to what you have to hand.

Serves 4

INGREDIENTS

900 g/2 lb unpeeled waxy potatoes, cut into wedges
25 g/1 oz/2 tbsp butter
1 red onion, halved and sliced
2 garlic cloves, crushed
25 g/1 oz/$\frac{1}{4}$ cup plain (all purpose) flour
600 ml/1 pint/$2\frac{1}{2}$ cups milk

397 g/14 oz can artichoke hearts in brine, drained and halved
150 g/$5\frac{1}{2}$ oz frozen mixed vegetables, thawed
125 g/$4\frac{1}{2}$ oz Gruyère cheese, grated
125 g/$4\frac{1}{2}$ oz mature (sharp) cheese, grated

50 g/$1\frac{3}{4}$ oz Gorgonzola cheese, crumbled
25 g/1 oz Parmesan cheese, grated
225 g/8 oz tofu (bean curd), sliced
2 tbsp chopped fresh thyme
salt and pepper
thyme sprigs, to garnish

1 Cook the potato wedges in a saucepan of boiling water for 10 minutes. Drain thoroughly.

2 Meanwhile, melt the butter in a saucepan. Add the sliced onion and garlic and fry gently for 2-3 minutes.

3 Stir the flour into the pan and cook for 1 minute. Gradually add the milk and bring to the boil, stirring constantly.

4 Reduce the heat and add the artichoke hearts, mixed vegetables, half of each of the 4 cheeses and the tofu (bean curd) to the pan, mixing well. Stir in the chopped fresh thyme and season with salt and pepper to taste.

5 Arrange a layer of parboiled potato wedges in the base of a shallow ovenproof dish. Spoon the vegetable mixture over the top and cover with the remaining potato wedges. Sprinkle the rest of the 4 cheeses over the top.

6 Cook in a preheated oven, 200°C/400°F/Gas Mark 6, for 30 minutes or until the potatoes are cooked and the top is golden brown. Serve the bake garnished with fresh thyme sprigs.

Hummus

Quick and easy to make, this dip features regularly on Mediterranean menus.
Serve it with fingers of pitta bread or vegetable sticks for dipping.

Makes about 700 g/1 lb 9 oz/scant 3 cups

INGREDIENTS

200 g/7 oz dried chick-peas
  (garbanzo beans)
2 large garlic cloves
7 tbsp extra-virgin olive oil

2½ tbsp tahini
1 tbsp lemon juice, or to taste
salt and pepper

TO GARNISH:
extra-virgin olive oil
paprika
fresh coriander (cilantro)

1 Place the chick-peas (garbanzo beans) in a large bowl. Pour in at least twice the volume of cold water to beans and leave to stand for at least 12 hours until they double in size.

2 Drain the chick-peas (garbanzo beans). Put them in a large flameproof casserole or saucepan and add twice the volume of water to beans. Bring to the boil and boil hard for 10 minutes, skimming the surface.

3 Lower the heat and leave to simmer for 1 hour, skimming the surface if necessary, or until the chick-peas (garbanzo beans) are tender. Meanwhile, cut the garlic cloves in half, remove the pale green or white cores and coarsely chop. Set aside.

4 Drain the chick-peas (garbanzo beans), reserving 4 tablespoons of the cooking liquid. Put the olive oil, garlic, tahini and lemon juice in a food processor and blend until a smooth paste forms.

5 Add the chick-peas (garbanzo beans) and pulse until they are finely ground but the hummus is still lightly textured. Add a little of the reserved cooking liquid if the mixture is too thick. Season with salt and pepper to taste.

6 Transfer to a bowl, cover with cling film (plastic wrap) and chill until ready to serve. To serve, drizzle with some olive oil, sprinkle a little paprika over and garnish with fresh coriander (cilantro).

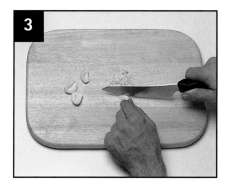

Baked Goat's Cheese Salad

Scrumptious hot goat's cheese and herb croûtes are served with a tossed leafy salad to make an excellent light snack, capturing Provençal flavours.

Serves 4

INGREDIENTS

250 g/9 oz mixed salad leaves, such
    as rocket (arugula), lamb's lettuce
    (corn salad) and chicory (endive)
12 slices French bread
extra-virgin olive oil, for brushing
12 thin slices of Provençal goat's
    cheese, such as Picodon

fresh herbs, such as rosemary, thyme
    or oregano, finely chopped
extra French bread, to serve

DRESSING:
6 tbsp extra-virgin olive oil
3 tbsp red wine vinegar
$\frac{1}{2}$ tsp sugar
$\frac{1}{2}$ tsp Dijon mustard
salt and pepper

1 To prepare the salad, rinse the leaves under cold water and pat dry with a tea towel (dish cloth). Wrap in paper towels and put in a plastic bag. Seal tightly and chill until required.

2 To make the dressing, place all the ingredients in a screw-top jar and shake until well blended. Season with salt and pepper to taste and shake again. Set aside while preparing the croûtes.

3 Toast the slices of bread on both sides until they are crisp. Brush a little olive oil on one side of each slice while still hot, so the oil is absorbed.

4 Place the croûtes on a baking (cookie) sheet and top each with a slice of cheese. Sprinkle the herbs over the cheese and drizzle with olive oil. Bake in a preheated oven at 180°C/350°F/Gas Mark 4 for 5 minutes.

5 While the croûtes are in the oven, place the salad leaves in a bowl. Shake the dressing again, pour it over the leaves and toss together. Equally divide the salad between 4 plates.

6 Transfer the hot croûtes to the salads. Serve at once with extra slices of French bread.

Spanish Tortilla

This simple recipe transforms the most humble ingredients – potatoes, eggs and an onion –
into a delicious thick omelette, ideal to serve as part of tapas, or as a light lunch.

Serves 6–8

INGREDIENTS

120 ml/4 fl oz/½ cup olive oil
600 g/1 lb 4 oz potatoes, sliced

1 large onion, sliced
1 large garlic clove, crushed

6 large eggs
salt and pepper

1 Heat a 25 cm/10 inch frying pan (skillet), preferably non-stick, over a high heat. Pour in the oil and heat. Lower the heat, add the potatoes, onion and garlic and cook for 15–20 minutes, stirring frequently, until the potatoes are tender.

2 Beat the eggs together in a large bowl and season generously with salt and pepper. Using a slotted spoon, transfer the potatoes and onion to the bowl of eggs. Pour the excess oil left in the frying pan (skillet) into a heatproof jug (pitcher), then scrape off the crusty bits from the base of the pan.

3 Reheat the pan. Add about 2 tablespoons of the reserved oil reserved in the jug (pitcher). Pour in the potato mixture, smoothing the vegetables into an even layer. Cook for about 5 minutes, shaking the pan occasionally, or until the base is set.

4 Shake the pan and use a spatula to loosen the side of the tortilla. Place a large plate over the pan. Carefully invert the tortilla on to the plate.

5 If you are not using a non-stick pan, add 1 tablespoon of the reserved oil to the pan and swirl around. Gently slide the

tortilla back into the pan, cooked-side up. Use the spatula to 'tuck down' the side. Continue cooking over medium heat for 3–5 minutes until set.

6 Remove the pan from the heat and slide the tortilla on to a serving plate. Leave to stand for at least 5 minutes before cutting. Serve hot, warm or at room temperature with salad.

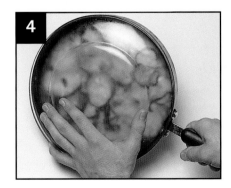

Mediterranean Monkfish

As any Mediterranean cook will tell you, some of the best seafood dishes are the simplest, and this recipe proves the point. It's ideal for serving in hot weather, when you want to spend as little time as possible in the kitchen.

Serves 4

INGREDIENTS

600 g/1 lb 4 oz vine-ripened cherry tomatoes, a mixture of yellow and red, if available

2 monkfish fillets, about 350 g/12 oz each

8 tbsp Pesto Sauce

salt and pepper
fresh basil sprigs, to garnish

---

1 Cut the tomatoes in half and scatter, cut-sides up, on the base of an ovenproof serving dish. Set aside.

2 Using your fingers, rub off the thin grey membrane that covers monkfish.

3 If the skin has not been removed, place the fish skin-side down on the work surface. Loosen enough skin at one end of the fillet so you can grip hold of it. Work from the front of the fillet to the back. Insert the knife, almost flat, and using a gentle sawing action, remove the skin.

Rinse the fillets well and dry with paper towels.

4 Place the fillets on top of the tomatoes, tucking the thin end under, if necessary, (see Cook's Tip). Spread 4 tablespoons of the pesto sauce over each fillet and season with pepper.

5 Cover the dish tightly with foil, shiny-side down. Place in a preheated oven at 230°C/450°F/Gas Mark 8 and roast for 16–18 minutes until the fish is cooked through, the flesh flakes easily and the tomatoes are dissolving into a thick sauce.

6 Adjust the seasoning, if necessary. Garnish with basil sprigs and serve at once with new potatoes.

COOK'S TIP

Monkfish fillets are often cut from the tail, which means one end is much thinner than the rest and prone to over-cooking. If you can't get fillets that are the same thickness, fold the thin end under for even cooking.

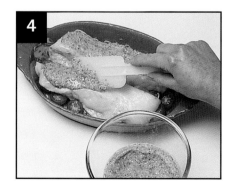

Golden Chicken Pilau

This is a simple version of a creamy textured and mildly spiced Indian pilau. Although there are lots of ingredients, there's very little preparation needed for this dish.

Serves 4

INGREDIENTS

60 g/2 oz/4 tbsp butter
8 skinless, boneless chicken thighs, cut into large pieces
1 medium onion, sliced
1 tsp ground turmeric
1 tsp ground cinnamon
250 g/9 oz/1 cup long grain rice

425 ml/^{3}/$_4$ pint/1^3/$_4$ cups natural (unsweetened) yogurt
60 g/2 oz/^{1}/$_3$ cup sultanas (golden raisins)
200 ml/7 fl oz/1 scant cup chicken stock
1 medium tomato, chopped

2 tbsp chopped fresh coriander (cilantro) or parsley
2 tbsp toasted coconut
salt and pepper
fresh coriander (cilantro), to garnish

1 Heat the butter in a heavy or non-stick pan and fry the chicken with the onion for about 3 minutes.

2 Stir in the turmeric, cinnamon, rice and seasoning and fry gently for 3 minutes.

3 Add the natural (unsweetened) yogurt, sultanas (golden raisins) and chicken stock and mix well. Cover and simmer for 10 minutes, stirring occasionally until the rice is tender and all the stock has been absorbed. Add more stock if the mixture becomes too dry.

4 Stir in the chopped tomato and fresh coriander (cilantro) or parsley.

5 Sprinkle the pilau with the toasted coconut and garnish with fresh coriander (cilantro).

COOK'S TIP

Long-grain rice is the most widely available and the cheapest rice. Basmati, with its slender grains and aromatic flavour is more expensive and should be used on special occasions if it is not affordable on a frequent basis. Rice, especially basmati, should be washed thoroughly under cold, running water before use.

Chicken with (Bell) Peppers & Black Bean Sauce

This tasty chicken stir-fry is quick and easy to make and is full of fresh flavours and crunchy vegetables.

Serves 4

INGREDIENTS

400 g/14 oz chicken breasts, sliced thinly
pinch of cornflour (cornstarch)
2 tbsp oil
1 garlic clove, crushed
1 tbsp black bean sauce
1 each small red and green (bell) pepper, cut into strips

1 red chilli, chopped finely
75 g/2³/4 oz/1 cup mushrooms, sliced
1 onion, chopped
6 spring onions (scallions), chopped
salt and pepper
fresh noodles, to serve

SEASONING:
¹/2 tsp salt
¹/2 tsp sugar
3 tbsp chicken stock
1 tbsp dark soy sauce
2 tbsp beef stock
2 tbsp rice wine
1 tsp cornflour (cornstarch), blended with a little rice wine

1 Put the chicken strips in a bowl. Add a pinch of salt and a pinch of cornflour (cornstarch) and cover with water. Leave for 30 minutes.

2 Heat 1 tbsp of the oil in a wok or frying pan (skillet) and stir-fry the chicken for 4 minutes. Transfer the chicken to a serving dish and clean the wok or pan.

3 Add the remaining oil to the wok or pan and add the garlic, black bean sauce, green and red (bell) peppers, chilli, mushrooms, onion and spring onions (scallions). Stir-fry the vegetables for 2 minutes then return the chicken strips to the wok.

4 Add the seasoning ingredients, fry for 3 minutes and thicken with a little of the cornflour (cornstarch) paste. Serve with fresh noodles.

COOK'S TIP

Black bean sauce can be found in specialist shops and in many supermarkets. Use dried noodles if you can't find fresh noodles.

Spicy Chicken Tortillas

Serve these easy-to-prepare tortillas to friends or as a special family supper.
The chicken filling has a mild, mellow spicy heat and a fresh salad makes a perfect accompaniment.

Serves 4

INGREDIENTS

2 tbsp oil
8 skinless, boneless chicken
   thighs, sliced
1 onion, chopped
2 garlic cloves, chopped
1 tsp cumin seeds, roughly crushed
2 large dried chillies, sliced

400 g/14 oz can tomatoes
400 g/14 oz can red kidney
   beans, drained
150 ml/¼ pint/⅔ cup chicken stock
2 tsp sugar
salt and pepper
lime wedges, to garnish

TO SERVE:
1 large ripe avocado
1 lime
8 soft tortillas
250 ml/9 fl oz/1 cup thick yogurt

1 Heat the oil in a large frying pan (skillet) or wok, add the chicken and fry for 3 minutes until golden. Add the onion and fry for 5 minutes, stirring until browned. Add the garlic, cumin and chillies, with their seeds, and cook for about 1 minute.

2 Add the tomatoes, kidney beans, stock, sugar and salt and pepper to taste. Bring to the boil, breaking up the tomatoes. Cover and simmer for 15 minutes.

Remove the lid and cook for 5 minutes, stirring occasionally until the sauce has thickened.

3 Halve the avocado, discard the stone and scoop out the flesh on to a plate. Mash the avocado with a fork. Cut half of the lime into 8 thin wedges. Squeeze the juice from the remaining lime over the avocado.

4 Warm the tortillas following the instructions on the packet.

Put two tortillas on each serving plate, fill with the chicken mixture and top with spoonfuls of avocado and yogurt. Garnish the tortillas with lime wedges.

VARIATION

For a vegetarian filling, replace the chicken with 400 g/14 oz canned pinto or cannellini beans and use vegetable stock instead of the chicken stock.

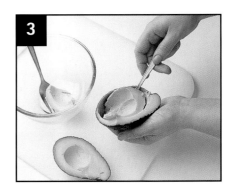

Neapolitan Pork Steaks

An Italian version of grilled pork steaks, this dish is easy to make and delicious to eat.

Serves 4

INGREDIENTS

2 tbsp olive oil
1 garlic clove, chopped
1 large onion, sliced
1 x 400 g/14 oz can tomatoes

2 tsp yeast extract
4 pork loin steaks, each about
 125 g/4^1/$_2$ oz
75 g/2^3/$_4$ oz black olives, pitted

2 tbsp fresh basil, shredded
freshly grated Parmesan cheese, to
 serve

1 Heat the oil in a large frying pan (skillet). Add the onions and garlic and cook, stirring, for 3–4 minutes or until they just begin to soften.

2 Add the tomatoes and yeast extract to the frying pan (skillet) and leave to simmer for about 5 minutes or until the sauce starts to thicken.

3 Cook the pork steaks, under a preheated grill (broiler), for 5 minutes on both sides, until the the meat is golden and cooked through. Set the pork steaks aside and keep warm.

4 Add the olives and fresh shredded basil to the sauce in the frying pan (skillet) and stir quickly to combine.

5 Transfer the steaks to warm serving plates. Top the steaks with the sauce, sprinkle with freshly grated Parmesan cheese and serve immediately.

COOK'S TIP

Parmesan is a mature and exceptionally hard cheese produced in Italy. You only need to add a little as it has a very strong flavour.

COOK'S TIP

There are many types of canned tomato available – for example plum tomatoes, or tomatoes chopped in water, or chopped sieved tomatoes (passata). The chopped variety are often canned with added flavours such as garlic, basil, onion, chilli and mixed herbs, and are a good storecupboard standby.

This is a Parragon Book
First published in 2003

Parragon
Queen Street House
4 Queen Street, Bath, BA1 1HE, UK

ISBN: 1-40540-832-4

Printed in China

NOTE

This book uses imperial and metric measurements. Follow the same units
of measurement throughout; do not mix imperial and metric. All spoon
measurements are level; teaspoons are assumed to be 5 ml and
tablespoons are assumed to be 15 ml. Unless otherwise stated, milk is
assumed to be whole milk, eggs and individual vegetables such as
potatoes are medium, and pepper is freshly ground black pepper.

The times given for each recipe are an approximate guide only because
the preparation times may differ according to the techniques used by
different people and the cooking times may vary as a result of the type of
oven used.

Recipes using raw or very lightly cooked eggs should be avoided by
infants, the elderly, pregnant women, convalescents and anyone suffering
from an illness.